Hmm...I Did Not Know That

1,000 random & interesting facts on a variety of subjects

By A.P. Holiday

****

Hmm...I Did Not Know That

Copyright © 2011 A.P. Holiday

Note: Facts are uncategorized and appear in random order. Hopefully each fact is as fresh and interesting as the one before.

****

Hmm...I Did Not Know That

1. An estimated one million earthworms live in one acre of soil.

2. Assassin John Wilkes Booth timed the shooting of Abraham Lincoln with a particularly humorous line in the play *Our American Cousin*, in the hope that the laughter of the audience would help mask the sound of the gunshot.

3. Monkeys are trained and employed as harvesters on large coconut plantations in Malaysia and Thailand.

4. Over a million cars are stolen each year in the United States.

5. A total of 438 people are killed in the course of the four "Rambo" movies.

6. The highest elevation in the Maldives is 7 feet, 7 inches above sea level, the lowest high point of any nation in the world.

7. Captive raccoons will often take food and dip it into water to "wash" it before eating.

8. After punching President Andrew Jackson in Virginia in 1833, a man named Robert B. Randolph was apprehended by a group of people that included "The Legend of Sleepy Hollow" author Washington Irving.

9. About six billion gallons of beer are brewed commercially in the U.S. every year.

10. Buzkashi, a sport popular in central Asia, is played by two teams mounted on horseback. The goal of the game is to transport a headless goat or calf carcass across a goal line.

11. The Beatles were once known as "Johnny and the Moondogs."

12. It is estimated that Alan Rufus, an 11th century British statesman, amassed a fortune that would have been the modern equivalent of 162 billion dollars during his lifetime.

13. The term "smart alec" is believed to be derived

from the nickname of a famous New York City pimp of the 1840s named Alec Hoag.

14. U.S. bombers dropped approximately 260 million bombs on the nation of Laos during the Vietnam War.

15. It is estimated that 14 new words are added to the English language every day.

16. Only 18 of the original 237 men who sailed out with Ferdinand Magellan's expedition to circumnavigate the globe actually completed the voyage.

17. Michael Cresta scored a record 830 points playing Scrabble during a tournament in 2006.

18. The equator lies across 14 different nations.

19. The average person uses an estimated 80-90 profanities each day.

20. Tabasco sauce was originally distributed in recycled glass cologne bottles.

21. Las Vegas casinos rake in an average of 9 billion dollars every year.

22. Peppercorns were found stuffed up the nose of the

mummified body of Egyptian Pharaoh Ramesses II.

23. R.J. Reynolds introduced the world's first packaged cigarettes, Camels, in 1913.

24. *Guinness Book of World Records* co-founder Ross McWhirter was assassinated by the IRA in 1975.

25. Badgers and coyotes have been known to cooperate with one another in concerted hunting trips.

26. Over 250,000 home runs have been hit in the history of Major League Baseball.

27. The Russian military used explosive-laden dogs to destroy German tanks during World War II.

28. The first paved road in the U.S. opened in 1795 and connected Lancaster, Pennsylvania and Philadelphia.

29. Both the White Castle and Pizza Hut restaurant chains were founded in Wichita, Kansas, in 1921 and 1958, respectively.

30. The widely used red food dye carmine is made from an acid produced by boiling a dried insect called the Cochineal.

31. An estimated 22 million people use marijuana on a daily basis.

32. The citizens of ancient Rome were the first to use a taxi service for transportation.

33. In 2009, more banks were robbed on Friday than any other day of the week.

34. It is estimated that there are over 6.8 billion people presently living on earth.

35. Frank Sinatra was thrown out of high school for bad behavior only 47 days after enrolling.

36. Employees of IBM have been the recipients of four Nobel Prizes.

37. The Boston Terrier can trace its roots back to a single dog known as Hooper's Judge, which was purchased by a Bostonian in 1870.

38. Bill Lear, founder of Lear Jets, helped invent the eight-track audio tape system.

39. 80% of the buildings in Warsaw, Poland, were destroyed during World War II.

40. There are more than 150 million water buffaloes

living on earth.

41. In 1983, Donald Davis ran backwards for a mile in a time of 6 minutes and 7.1 seconds, a world record for the backwards mile.

42. The main ingredient of the Polish soup czernina is duck blood.

43. Point Barrow, Alaska, is the northernmost point in the United States.

44. Early European shower systems allowed the same water to be used over and over again for multiple bathers.

45. The athletic teams at Illinois' Freeport High School are known as "The Pretzels."

46. The Snickers bar was first sold as the "Gooey Chocolatey Peanut Buttery Fun Bar."

47. Five of the seven poorest per-capita counties in the United States are located in South Dakota.

48. The word "poppycock" descends from a Dutch word meaning "soft feces."

49. The South Korean national junior hockey team

defeated the Thai team 92-0 during a tournament game in 1998.

50. About 70% of the people bitten by rattlesnakes are male.

51. The largest hailstone ever measured fell in Vivian, South Dakota, in 2010. It was 18 inches in diameter and weighed nearly two pounds.

52. Slavery in the United States began upon the arrival of a ship bearing 20 African captives in Virginia in 1619.

53. A weapon called the Apache revolver, which became popular with French criminals in the early 20th century, was a combination pistol, brass knuckles and knife.

54. *Peanuts* character Snoopy was originally to be called Sniffy.

55. The Seawise Giant, at over 1,500 feet in length, and with a capacity of over 642,000 tons, was the largest ship ever built.

56. In Romanian, the name Dracula means "son of the dragon."

57. Thirty-two carrier pigeons were awarded medals

by the United Kingdom for their service in World Wars I and II.

58. Slavery was outlawed in Rhode Island in 1652.

59. The Bullenbeisser breed of German Bulldog, which was bred with the English Bulldog to form the Boxer breed, is now extinct.

60. The Georgia Tech football team racked up 1,620 rushing yards in its 222-0 destruction of Cumberland College in 1916.

61. Mosquitoes infect more than 700 million people with various diseases each year.

62. A butler, trained at one of a small number of specialized butlering schools, can expect to earn a starting salary of $50,000-60,000 per year upon graduation.

63. The tallest man-made structure in the United States is the 2,063-foot tall KVLY/KTHI TV tower located near Blanchard, North Dakota.

64. The corpse of Pope Formusus was dug up and put on trial by Pope Stephen VI (VII) for crimes committed while Formusus was still alive. The corpse was found guilty and thrown into the Tiber River.

65. The first Big Mac was served in a Pittsburgh area McDonalds in 1968.

66. Cornelius Vanderbilt never set foot on the campus of the Nashville university which bears his name, and which was endowed by his one million dollar gift in 1873.

67. Two U.S. vice presidents, Dick Cheney and Aaron Burr, have shot someone while serving as vice president of the United States.

68. There are over 13,000 taxis operating in New York City.

69. Grey Poupon mustard is not widely available in France. The American version is made from mustard seeds grown in Canada.

70. The Brazen Head, founded in Dublin in 1198, is Ireland's oldest pub.

71. Marlon Brando was expelled from high school for riding a motorcycle through the hallway.

72. Of all the money spent by militaries in the world, the U.S. spends about 43 percent.

73. During the construction of the Hoover Dam, the Colorado River was diverted through four tunnels cut

through the rock on either si[

74. Russell Stover and busin
Nelson introduced the "Eski

brigadier ge
the last Ci
finally

75. Alfred Nobel's younger
by a nitroglycerin explosio.. ... __
family's explosives factories in 1964.

76. It takes the planet of Saturn about 29 Earth years to completely orbit the sun.

77. Batman creator Bob Kane cited Scottish soldier Robert Bruce and American Revolutionary War General "Mad" Anthony Wayne as his sources for naming Batman's alter ego Bruce Wayne.

78. Former Guns N' Roses guitarist Slash's real name is Saul Hudson.

79. Salicylic acid, the active ingredient in aspirin, has been obtained from tree bark for use in pain relief since the beginning of recorded history.

80. Musician Kris Kristofferson, as a college athlete, appeared in Sports Illustrated magazine's "Faces in the Crowd" section because of his exploits on the football field.

81. Stand Watie, a Cherokee Indian leader and

eral for the Confederate army, became
vil War general to surrender when he
stood down in June of 1865.

82. The first U.S. income tax was instituted in 1862 to help fund the Civil War.

83. Bernhard Stroh, the founder of Stroh's Beer, started out selling beer door-to-door from a wheelbarrow in Detroit in the 1850s.

84. Only about 9,000 DeLorean automobiles were manufactured during the company's brief existence in the 1980s.

85. Banker and industrialist J.P. Morgan cancelled, at the last moment, his trip on the ill-fated HMS Titanic in 1912.

86. A Wendy's restaurant in Columbus, Ohio, began utilizing the world's first modern drive-through window in 1971.

87. The Pacific Ocean covers over 63 million square miles.

88. The U.S. Air Force became an official branch of the U.S. military in 1947. Before that date, the Air Force was part of the U.S. Army.

89. Willis Carrier built the first modern air conditioner to cool printing presses in New York, in 1902.

90. The state song of Alabama is "Alabama."

91. There have been over 20 assassinations and/or assassination attempts on sitting U.S. presidents.

92. The gluteus maximus is the largest muscle in the human body.

93. Edgar Allan Poe married his 13-year old cousin Virginia in 1835.

94. Only about 40% of a Pringles brand snack is actual potato.

95. A cable car system used to transport metal ores in Sweden ran for over 60 miles, making it the longest aerial tramway ever operated.

96. Roman Emperor Commodus often fought as a gladiator, although most of his opponents were inferior or impaired.

97. Reykjavik, Iceland, is the world's northernmost national capital city.

. Hagar the Horrible cartoonist Dik Browne esigned the logo for Chiquita Bananas.

99. The world's first roller coasters, called "Russian Mountains," were built near St. Petersburg, Russia, in the 15th century.

100. Nicaraguan sign language was developed spontaneously in the 1970s and 1980s by deaf children who attended newly built schools for the deaf.

101. The fastest typist ever recorded, Stella Pajunas-Garnand, typed at a rate of 216 words per minute.

102. Early wine bottles were capped with oil-soaked rags before cork stoppers came into use.

103. Some "social spiders" of South America live in colonies of up to 50,000 spiders.

104. The ancient Greeks covered their mouths when yawning to prevent their souls from escaping their bodies.

105. Pennsylvanian Dean Lindsay made a legal claim for all objects in outer space in 1936.

106. Pandiculation is the act of yawning and stretching at the same time.

107. It is believed there were more th[...] billionaires living in 2010, of whom [...] North America.

108. The world's population has bee[...] growth since the 1400s.

109. Papua, New Guinea, has the world's highest percentage (29%) of marijuana users in the world.

110. Blues legend Son House was sentenced to fifteen years in prison for killing a man who was on a shooting spree in a Mississippi juke joint in 1928.

111. U.S. President Richard Nixon was the first president to visit all 50 states.

112. The Black Death is estimated to have killed more than 100 million people in the 13th century.

113. The world's first traffic lights were installed in London in 1868.

114. Octopi are genetically wired to die soon after mating.

115. The CBS television network mushroomed to popularity after the cigar-making Paley family of Philadelphia purchased the network in order to advertise their line of cigars in 1928.

German Adolf Fick developed the first contact
ns in 1887.

117. Students at Baylor University in Waco, Texas
can get a free ice cream float made with Dr. Pepper
soda at the student union from 3 to 4 pm every
Tuesday during the school year.

118. Ancient Romans used an early form of air
conditioning: they ran cool water from aqueducts
through the walls of their houses.

119. Over 15 million Junior Mints candies are
produced every day.

120. The Palace of Parliament in Bucharest, Romania,
is the world's heaviest building.

121. Over 45 million dollars was stolen in the United
States in 2009.

122. Peru fought for its independence from Spain for
15 years.

123. In the late 19th century, the University of
Nebraska athletic teams were known as the
Bugeaters.

124. The motion picture company Warner Bros.
began as a single movie theater opened by four Polish

brothers in New Castle, Pennsylvania, in 1903.

125. Pig and badger hair was used for bristles in the first mass-produced toothbrushes, manufactured in Europe in the 19th century.

126. True balsamic vinegar must be aged for a minimum of 12 years.

127. In the 1930s, consumers used credit cards made of sheet metal.

128. After fatally knifing Ernesto Miranda in 1976, an unknown assailant was read his "Miranda rights," which were named after his victim.

129. The first commercial beer brewery in America opened in Manhattan in 1632.

130. More than 35,000 episodes of ESPN's Sportcenter have been aired since its launch in 1979.

131. There have been 133 different colors of Crayola crayons.

132. The Emancipation Proclamation freed captive slaves but did not outlaw the practice of slavery.

133. Drug and explosive-sniffing mice are used by

Israeli security personnel.

134. As a teen, television host Johnny Carson performed as an amateur magician known as "Carsoni."

135. The first bungee jumps were made, illegally, from the Clifton Suspension Bridge in Bristol, England in 1979.

136. Babe Ruth learned the trade of tailoring before beginning his Major League Baseball career.

137. Pet dogs are descended from the domesticated grey wolf.

138. Ted Turner owns over two million acres of land in the United States.

139. British runner Robert Garside is the first person to run around the world. His journey took over five years and covered some 35,000 miles.

140. Neither Orville nor Wilbur Wright received a high school diploma.

141. Winston Churchill was the first person ever to be made an honorary citizen of the United States.

142. Wrigley's chewing gum was originally included as a freebie to go along with packages of the company's baking powder. The gum soon surpassed the powder's popularity, and the company began producing chewing gum as its main product.

143. The Federal Building/Post Office in downtown Texarkana is located in both Arkansas and Texas.

144. Elvis Presley had a twin brother who died at birth.

145. Heroin was available for purchase as an over-the-counter drug in Germany in the late 19th century.

146. Cumin is known to reduce flatulence in humans.

147. Ancient residents of cold, icy areas were known to build ice skates out of animal bones in order to traverse large ice-covered areas more quickly.

148. Barbie's full name is Barbara Millicent Roberts and she is a native of Wisconsin.

149. Cork is harvested by shearing the bark from the cork oak tree every 9 to 12 years.

150. Jackie Robinson's brother, Matthew Robinson, finished second to Jesse Owens in the 200 meter event at the 1936 Summer Olympics in Berlin.

151. The Apollo 11 landing craft spent 21 hours and 31 minutes on the surface of the moon in 1969.

152. The world's first escalator was put into use at Coney Island, New York, in 1896.

153. There are 43,000 miles of phone wire inside the Willis (Sears) Tower in Chicago.

154. William Shakespeare was married at the age of 18 to 26-year-old Anne Hathaway, who was three months pregnant with their first child.

155. The weather station at Tamarack, California, received over 32 feet of snow in the month of January, 1911.

156. Pinball machines were banned in Los Angeles and New York City during the 1930s.

157. Pound for pound, the diminutive Shetland Pony is the world's strongest horse breed.

158. Almost 500 billion Oreo cookies have been consumed since they were introduced in 1912.

159. The world's longest stairway, located near Spiez, Switzerland, uses 11,674 steps to climb 5,476 ft/1,669 m up the side of a mountain.

160. During World War II, the United States military unsuccessfully attempted a program to use bats to spread incendiary bombs onto enemy targets.

161. The QWERTY style keyboard was developed by Christopher Sholes in Milwaukee in the 1870s.

162. The old German translation for the word "pumpernickel" bread means "goblin fart."

163. Gillette Stadium, home of the NFL's New England Patriots, with a seating capacity of 68,756, can hold 52,458 more people than live in the city in which it is located: Foxborough, Massachusetts.

164. A horse fly can reach flying speeds of up to 90 mph/145 kmh.

165. The Eurasian nation of Georgia has the world's highest literacy rate.

166. China and Russia each share borders with 14 other nations, the most in the world.

167. Tennessee's Memphis International Airport handles more cargo tonnage per year than any other airport in the world.

168. Lieutenant Henry Farley is believed to be the soldier responsible for the first shots of the U.S. Civil

War. Farley ordered two mortars discharged at Fort Sumter, South Carolina, at 4:30 a.m. on April 12, 1861.

169. Harry Reese, a former Hershey's employee, developed Reese's Peanut Butter Cups in his basement.

170. The word "dude" is defined as a well-dressed man who lives in a large city.

171. Margarine was invented in France in 1869 as a cheap substitute for butter.

172. Movie monster Godzilla's name is a combination of the Japanese words for gorilla and whale.

173. 16 million dollars worth of food stamps were stolen in the U.S. in 2009.

174. The *Washington Post* became the first U.S. newspaper to publish seven days a week when it began a Sunday edition in 1880.

175. Slavery was abolished in Japan in the 16th century, by Russia in 1723, by Canada in 1803, by Mexico in 1810 and the United States in 1865.

176. Vincent Van Gogh shot himself at the age of 37.

177. Frenchman Stephane Mifsud held his breath underwater for 11 minutes and 35 seconds in 2009, a world record.

178. It takes an average of 12-24 trees to make a ton of writing paper.

179. The U.S. federal government employs about two million civilian employees.

180. George Takai, who played Sulu on Star Trek, lived in Japanese internment camps in California and Arkansas as a child.

181. Twitter users send over 50 million "tweets" every day.

182. John Wilkes Booth's older brother, Edwin, supported the Union during the Civil War.

183. Wendy's founder Dave Thomas did not earn his high school diploma until 1993, at the age of 61.

184. An estimated 150,000 to 246,000 people died as a result of the atomic bombings of Hiroshima and Nagasaki, Japan, in 1945.

185. Over 70 Nobel laureates attended or have taught at the Massachusetts Institute of Technology (MIT) in Boston.

186. Meriwether Clark, Jr., the grandson of William Clark of Lewis and Clark fame, was the founder of Churchill Downs, the home of the Kentucky Derby.

187. Richard Sears, who went on to found Sears, Roebuck and Company, was a childhood friend of Alonzo Wilder, the future husband of writer Laura Ingalls Wilder.

188. Lyme Disease is named for Lyme, Connecticut, where a number of early cases of the disease popped up in the 1970s.

189. A record 452 point match by Australian Cricket legend Donald Bradman so impressed the losing team that they carried him off the field on their shoulders.

190. Nearly four million East Germans defected to West Berlin before the construction of the Berlin Wall in 1961.

191. Early striptease acts featured women disrobing while pretending to try and find a bee in their clothing.

192. American John Gorrie inadvertently invented ice cubes when he built a refrigerator for cooling air in 1844.

193. Author Jack Kerouac earned scholarship offers

to play football at Boston College, Notre Dame and Columbia. He played running back at Columbia before an injury helped to end his athletic career.

194. About half the residents of Florida's Miami-Dade County were born in a country other than the United States.

195. During World War II, more than 100 million pounds of Spam was sent to feed Allied troops around the world.

196. Aluminum is the most common active ingredient in antiperspirants.

197. Chicago's O'Hare Airport was named in honor of U.S. Navy fighter pilot and Medal of Honor recipient Butch O'Hare.

198. When revolutionary Samuel Adams was elected to the Continental Congress in 1774, he was so broke that he had to borrow money and clothes from friends to make the trip to Philadelphia.

199. A shopping cart can cost as much as $150.

200. Every mile of the Mason-Dixon Line was marked with stones imported from England.

201. Author Ian Fleming, an avid bird-watcher,

named his famous fictional spy, 007, after prominent American ornithologist James Bond.

202. The population center of the United States is located about a half mile southwest of the town of Plato, Missouri.

203. Elmer Doolin, the founder of Fritos corn chips, paid a San Antonio chef $100 for the original Fritos recipe in the 1930s.

204. Ngwenyama Sobhuza II, after ascending to leadership of Swaziland at the age of only a few months, ruled the nation for the next 82 years.

205. During his senior year at Syracuse, Jim Brown was an all-American in both football and lacrosse.

206. After using the toilet, ancient Romans cleaned themselves with a single communal sponge, which was cleaned with salt water between uses.

207. There are no woodpeckers in Australia or New Zealand.

208. There are 40 U.S. cities with populations greater than that of the entire state of Wyoming.

209. *Naked Lunch* author William Burroughs' grandfather, also named William Burroughs, made a

fortune after developing the modern add

210. Astronauts Fred Haise, James Lovel.
Swigert are the three humans who have tr
farthest from earth. The astronauts were an estimated
248,000+ miles away from earth as they flew around
the dark side of the moon in 1970.

211. The ZIP in the US. Postal Service term "ZIP
code" stands for "zone improvement plan."

212. A broken wedding engagement between the
daughter of the Emperor of Rome and the son of the
King of the Vandals helped to trigger the monumental
sacking of Rome by the Vandals in 422.

213. It cost 375 million dollars to construct the
Panama Canal.

214. About 30% of the total German military was
killed fighting World War II.

215. The three beverages most commonly consumed
in the world are, in order of popularity: water, tea and
beer.

216. Dolphins have been known to use sponges to
protect their snouts from damage while searching for
food.

217. An estimated 450 million people heard Neil Armstrong say "That's one small step for (a) man, one giant leap for mankind" when he set foot on the moon in 1969.

218. Cellophane tape was invented by American Richard Drew in 1930.

219. 85% of the world's horseradish is grown in the state of Illinois.

220. There is no preceding "The" in the English name of the European nation Ukraine.

221. Wal Mart, K-Mart and Target were all founded in 1962.

222. Australia's Highway 1, at over 9,000 miles, is the longest highway in the world.

223. Charles Richter, developer of the Richter scale, was an avid nudist.

224. On January 12, 2010, there was snow on the ground in every U.S. state except Florida.

225. Russia has over 21 million people serving in the armed forces.

226. Sauerkraut is a Thanksgiving dinner staple in many households in the Baltimore, Maryland area.

227. Lee Harvey Oswald murdered Dallas police officer J.D. Tippit approximately 40 minutes after John F. Kennedy was shot.

228. The Uros, an indigenous people of South America, live on a series of 42 man-made islands in Lake Titicaca. The islands were built by binding together bundles of dried reeds.

229. The United States has detonated over 1,000 nuclear bombs since testing began in 1945.

230. There are more than 30 duplications of the Eiffel Tower located around the world.

231. 266 people live in the community of Hell, Michigan.

232. Financial company American Express began as a mail delivery business in Albany, New York, in 1850.

233. The band Pink Floyd was named after the first names of two blues musicians found in the record collection of band member Syd Barrett.

234. American novelist Winston Churchill was born in St. Louis in 1871, three years before the more well-

taple in area.

Churchill was born. The two
ed name, met and maintained

Postal Service operates the
et of vehicles in the world.

236. The Airbus A380 airliner can hold up to 853 passengers.

237. Legendary racehorse Secretariat set race records at the Kentucky Derby and the Belmont stakes during his epic Triple Crown season of 1973. Both records still stand today.

238. Italian Alessandro Volta invented the electrical battery in 1800.

239. Pine cones were originally known as pineapples.

240. Musicians Norah Jones, Pat Boone, Roy Orbison, Meatloaf and Don Henley all attended the University of North Texas.

241. The largest bubble gum bubble ever recorded was 23 inches in diameter.

242. The classic painting American Gothic, by Grant Wood, features a father and a daughter standing in front of a farmhouse, not a husband and wife, as

many people assume.

243. Before coming to power in Germany, Adolph Hitler lived for a time in a homeless shelter.

244. Wintergreen is highly toxic if ingested in large amounts.

245. Croquet was an event at the 1900 Summer Olympics.

246. U.S. President William McKinley, after being shot by assassin Leon Czolgolz, yelled "Don't let them hurt him!" to the throng of people beating the subdued gunman.

247. A badger can run at a speed of up to 19 mph.

248. The Plymouth Iron Windmill Company of Michigan began giving away BB guns with each windmill purchased by customers. The guns were so popular that the company stopped manufacturing windmills to concentrate on BB guns, and later became the Daisy Airgun Company.

249. Early Persian architects used "wind catcher" towers on the tops of buildings to direct the prevailing breezes down and through houses in order to cool them.

ghest income tax rate in the

ack Whale weighs around

252. The annual Prize banquet did not take place in 1979, when Peace Prize recipient Mother Theresa stated that the money used on the dinner could be better spent. The $7,000 dollars originally intended for the event was instead used to feed 20,000 needy people.

253. One acre of poppies will yield 6-11 pounds of raw opium.

254. The first crossword puzzle appeared in an Italian magazine in 1890.

255. Inventor Norm Larsen was successful in his 40th try at finding a spray to displace water and prevent erosion. Larsen named the fluid WD-40, or "Water Displacement-40th attempt."

256. Over 300,000 soldiers are believed to have died during the Battle of Saisu, a conflict between Chinese and Korean forces in the year 612.

257. The numerically highest postal ZIP code in the United States is 99950, in Ketchikan, Alaska.

258. Military flamethrowers were first used by soldiers in the 1st century AD.

259. The fastest a person had driven a land-based vehicle by the year 1898 was just over 39 miles per hour.

260. There were an estimated four million people living in slavery in the United States in 1860.

261. German Karl Dobermann bred the first Dobermann Pinscher dogs to help protect him in his job as a government tax collector in the 1890s.

262. Sugar Daddy caramel pops were originally called "Poppa Suckers."

263. The lowest point on earth, not located beneath an ocean, is the Bentley Sub-glacial Trench in Antarctica, which lies 8,382 feet below sea level.

264. About 15% of the total area of Manitoba, Canada, is water.

265. The largest hotel in the world is Las Vegas' MGM Grand, which has over 7,300 rooms.

266. Mexican actor and director Emilio Fernandez was the model for the Academy Award (Oscar) statue.

267. Irish brewer Arthur Guinness signed a 9,000-year lease on the St. James Gate Brewery when he began his beer brewing business in 1759.

268. Paris, France, is the most popular tourist destination in the world.

269. Many historians believe that ancient Roman politician Marcus Licinius Crassus was the wealthiest man in history. His net worth is believed to have been equal to the entire treasury of Rome.

270. 7-Up soda was originally touted as a cure for hangovers.

271. The town of Foc-Foc on the island of Reunion in the Indian Ocean received a record 1,825 mm/71.9 inches of rain in a 24 hour period in 1966.

272. Crazy Horse was shot in the jaw in an altercation with the spurned former husband of his first wife.

273. The family of Henry David Thoreau was one of the first pencil manufacturers in the United States.

274. John D. Rockefeller became the world's first billionaire in 1916.

275. The first metal baseball bat was patented in 1924.

276. Nineteen people have been awarded more than one U.S. Medal of Honor.

277. Over 13,000 people were murdered in the United States in 2009.

278. The first commercial airline flight in the U.S. took place in Florida in 1914.

279. LSD is produced from a chemical derived from a fungus that grows on grain, especially rye.

280. Dartboards used to be made from solid blocks of wood. The boards were soaked in water to reduce the size of the holes made by the darts.

281. In the early 19th century, U.S. vice president and former senator from Kentucky Richard Mentor Johnson had a long-term affair with a mullatto former slave named Julia Chinn, whom he openly considered his common-law wife.

282. The jock strap was invented, for use by bicycle messengers who battled rocky streets, by C.F. Bennett of Chicago in 1874.

283. A giant tortoise named Adwaita died in 2006 at an estimated age of 255 years.

284. Hillary Clinton's brother, Hugh Rodham, was a

backup quarterback for the Penn State football team in the late 1960s and early 1970s.

285. Over 350 million Rubik's Cubes have been sold since they were introduced in 1980.

286. Gatling gun inventor Richard Gatling claimed that he invented the machine gun in order to reduce combat deaths.

287. John Grisham's debut novel, *A Time to Kill*, was rejected by 28 publishers before it went to print in 1989.

288. Superman was modeled on swashbuckling 1920s movie star Douglas Fairbanks.

289. In 1871, Uranus became the first planet discovered with a telescope; before that time, it was believed to be a star.

290. The Chinese restaurant staple General Tso's Chicken is believed to have originated in New York City in the 1970s.

291. 31 counties in the United States use the name Washington County, the most of any county name.

292. The first printed advertisement in history, an ad for a book, was made in England in 1472.

293. The United States is about 3.7 million square miles in area.

294. Moroccan King Moulay Ismil Ibn Sharif fathered an estimated 800-1000 children during his lifetime.

295. Iceland is the only member of NATO without a standing army.

296. A centipede can have anywhere from 20 to 300 legs.

297. The Chevrolet vehicle brand was founded by a Swiss-born race car driver and vehicle designer named Louis Chevrolet.

298. The first commercial microwave oven was built in 1947.

299. The world's oldest still-operating university is the University of Bologna in Italy, which was founded in 1088.

300. Loving County, Texas is the United States' least populated county, with a population hovering at around 70 people.

301. Foot Locker sporting footwear stores are the only remaining branch of the once ubiquitous five-

and-dime chain Woolworth's.

302. A baby rattlesnake is on its own immediately after birth.

303. Jim Thorpe won two Olympic gold medals, played Major League Baseball, NFL football and professional basketball during his athletic career.

304. Calcium carbonate, the active ingredient in many antacids, is the main substance in snail shells and pearls.

305. Chicagoan Sebastian Hinton invented the jungle gym in 1920.

306. There are four nations in South America in which Spanish is not the official language: Brazil (Portuguese), French Guiana (French), Guyana (English) and Suriname (Dutch).

307. The mold in blue cheese is formed from the introduction of the bacteria penicillium.

308. Entertainer Josephine Baker won the French Croix de guerre (Cross of war) for her efforts in helping the French Resistance during World War II.

309. In 2006, business giant Warren Buffett donated over 30 billion dollars to the Gates Foundation.

310. The Confederate warship "Alabama" was sunk by Union warships in June, 1864, just off the coast of Cherbourg, France.

311. By sealing its nasal passages shut, a Sea Lion can stay underwater for up to 15 minutes.

312. The Methuselah tree in eastern California is believed to be 4,842 years old.

313. Both German and Japanese forces attacked the mainland of Australia during World War II.

314. Daredevil Evel Knievel broke 35 bones and spent 36 months in the hospital during his stunt career.

315. In 2010, 21 of the 50 U.S. state governors were born in a state other than the one they governed.

316. In 1925, at the height of Prohibition, there were believed to be up to 100,000 speakeasies in the United States.

317. Leprechauns were originally described as wearing red clothes instead of green.

318. The indentation between a persons upper lip and nose is called a philtrum.

319. The United States' most widely read newspaper, the *Wall Street Journal*, was founded by Charles Bergstresser, Charles Dow and Edward Jones in New York in 1889.

320. There are believed to be over 100 million AK-47 rifles in use around the world.

321. Louis Armstrong's nickname "Satchmo" was short for his other nickname "Satchelmouth."

322. A woman named Ann Hodges was struck by a meteorite while sitting on her sofa in Alabama in 1954.

323. In 1799, France became the first nation to officially adopt the metric system.

324. Cashews must be roasted outdoors because of the highly toxic fumes that are produced during the process.

325. The first open heart surgery was performed in Montgomery, Alabama, in 1902.

326. Alexander Hamilton and his son Philip were both killed in seperate duels at the Weehawken dueling ground in New Jersey.

327. Early mirrors were made of polished stone, such

as obsidian.

328. There are over one million students in the New York City School District.

329. A bolt of lightning can reach a temperature of 30,000 C/54,000 F.

330. The Suzuki Motor Corporation began as a weaving loom manufacturer in 1909.

331. There are an estimated 312 million Americans.

332. Dolphins use their lower jaw for hearing.

333. The southernmost national capital city is Wellington, New Zealand.

334. J&B Scotch is a mixture of 42 different kinds of scottish whiskies.

335. The United States consumes about 44% of the world's gasoline.

336. Ancient Romans took their dirty togas to commercial dry cleaners.

337. The first color photograph was taken in 1861.

338. Frenchwoman Jeanne Louise Calment died in 1997 at the age of 122 years old; she is the longest-lived person on record in modern times.

339. Denver International Airport is larger than the nation of Monaco.

340. There are somewhere between 3,000-6,000 languages spoken on earth today.

341. The American Civil War killed about 2% of the total U.S. population at the time.

342. The largest known dinosaur, the Giraffatitan, is believed to have been 37 feet tall and weighed 130,000 lbs.

343. 20% of the earth's land is located in Africa.

344. The first property insurance company in the United States was founded by Benjamin Franklin in Philadelphia in 1752.

345. A tunnel for pedestrians was built beneath the Euphrates River by the Babylonians in the 13th century.

346. Canadians Scott Abbott and Chris Haney invented the board game *Trivial Pursuit* after finding that they did not have enough tiles to play a game of *Scrabble*.

347. There are over five billion cell phones in use around the world today.

348. 1972 was the last year that a human set foot on the moon.

349. On a clear day, visitors at the top of the Willis (formerly the Sears) Tower can see 50 miles in all directions.

350. A California redwood tree can stand up to 379 feet in height.

351. Johnny Cash was named J.R. Cash because his parents could not agree on a first name.

352. The Star Carr house, near Scarborough, North Yorkshire, UK, at over 10,500 years old, is the oldest known house in the United Kingdom.

353. The U.S. used over 5,000 "war dogs" during the Vietnam War.

354. Jockey Alonzo Clayton became the youngest Kentucky Derby winning jockey in 1892, when he won the crown at age 15.

355. Wal Mart founder Sam Walton's first job out of college was as a management trainee at J.C. Penney.

356. Drinking coffee was prohibited in parts of Asia during the 16th century.

357. There are 276 U.S. cities with populations over 100,000.

358. Polish revolutionary Tadeusz Kosciusko has over two dozen place-names in the U.S., thousands of streets, squares and statues in Europe, and a mountain in Australia named in his honor.

359. Concrete is the most used man made material in the world.

360. Koi fish have been known to live for over 200 years.

361. Over 100,000 people have been killed while working as coal miners in the history of the United States.

362. It took Michelangelo four years to paint the ceiling of the Sistine Chapel.

363. About 40,000 trees are used to produce a season's worth of Louisville Slugger baseball bats.

364. British pilots John Alcock and Arthur Brown completed the first transatlantic flight in 1919, eight years before Charles Lindbergh's first solo crossing.

365. Roman gladiators often wore gloves, called Cestus, which were equipped with metal plates or spikes in order to increase damage to opponents.

366. There are an estimated 400 million dogs living on earth.

367. India's Gul Mohammed is the smallest person in recorded history. Mohommed measured in at 22 inches tall and weighed 38 pounds.

368. More than 900 million people travel as international tourists each year.

369. Frenchman Nicephore Niepce took the world's first known photograph in 1825. Niepce is also credited with developing the world's first internal combustion engine in 1807.

370. Large groups of fireflies in such places as Malaysia, the Philippines and the southeastern United States, have been known to illuminate in unison.

371. The Battle of New Orleans took place after the actual end of the War of 1812.

372. Football legend Jim Brown's Long Island high school basketball scoring record of 38 points per game was broken by baseball legend Carl Yastrzemski.

373. More than two million people attended the funeral procession of French author Victor Hugo in Paris in 1885.

374. A canned sardine can be one of 21 different species of fish.

375. The Guinea Pig was first domesticated as a food source in the Andes mountains of South America.

376. Kickball was invented by Nicholas Seuss in Cincinnati, Ohio, in 1917.

377. The first corporation chartered in America was Harvard College in 1636.

378. The highest ever score on the *Asteroids* arcade game is 43,336,440.

379. The 1883 eruption of Indonesia's Mount Krakatoa was so violent that the explosion was heard over 2,000 miles away in Australia.

380. There are an estimated 22,000 different species of ants.

381. Football legend Red Grange earned 16 varsity letters while playing four sports in high school in Wheaton, Illinois.

382. Great Britain repaid the United States 15.5 million dollars in reparations for damages inflicted on U.S. shipping operations by supporting Confederate warships during the U.S. Civil War.

383. A female Killer Whale can live up to 90 years.

384. The odds of winning the Powerball lottery jackpot are roughly 1 in 195 million.

385. An estimated 300,00 to 1.5 million people were killed in sacrificial rituals during the reign of the Aztec empire in Mexico.

386. Sewing machine inventor Elias Howe also patented an early version of the zipper in 1851.

387. Early flashlights could only be shined in short bursts.

388. Nearly 12% of all Americans live in California.

389. The letters E, T and A, in that order, are the three most frequently used letters in the English language.

390. Over 16 million Americans served in the U.S. military during World War II.

391. Teton County, Wyoming has the highest average income of any county in the United States, at $132,728 per capita.

392. A peregrine falcon can reach a speed of over 200 miles per hour.

393. Wal-Mart employs over two million people worldwide.

394. A typical wolf pack in the wild is a nuclear family, meaning it is made up of two parents and their offspring.

395. The U.S. military had a budget of over 690 billion dollars in 2010.

396. The average life expectancy in Swaziland, Africa, is only 31.88 years.

397. Civil War soldiers sometimes melted lead bullets to make "brass knuckles."

398. The largest road-legal trucks in Australia can be up to 175 feet long and carry a payload of up to 361,558 pounds.

399. John D. Rockefeller donated 8.5 million dollars to purchase the land for the construction of the U.N. headquarters in New York City.

400. A flea can jump up to two hundred times its own body length, the equivalent of a 5' 9" human jumping 1,150 feet, or almost a quarter mile.

401. The world's first satellite, the Sputnik I, launched in 1957, was about the size of a basketball and took roughly 90 minutes to complete an entire orbit of the earth.

402. At a price of over 1.5 million dollars, the Bugatti Veyron is the most expensive production automobile in the world.

403. In some Asian countries, a barber's pole is used to advertise a house of prostitution.

404. Licorice is often used to enhance the taste and smoothness of tobacco.

405. A large colony of parakeets, descended from escaped birds, lives in the wild near Brooklyn College in New York.

406. *Charlie and the Chocolate Factory* author Roald Dahl was an ace fighter pilot and intelligence agent for Great Britain during World War II.

407. Some of the finer stone blocks used in the construction of the Egyptian Pyramids were transported in from over 500 miles away.

408. Doc Holliday's wife was known as "Big Nose Kate."

409. Sixty-one graduates of the UK's Cambridge University are Nobel laureates, the most of any university in the world.

410. Explorer Meriwether Lewis was accidentally shot by a Lewis & Clark expedition member during an elk hunt in 1806.

411. Nearly 4,000 Kamikaze pilots flew to their deaths in suicide attacks during World War II.

412. California's Los Angeles County, at 9.9 million people, is the most highly populated county in the United States.

413. Book publishing giant Simon & Shuster began business as a publisher of crossword puzzles.

414. Richard Halliburton, an American, was charged

a toll of 36 cents to swim the Panama Canal in 1928.

415. The world's busiest Wal-Mart store is located in Rapid City, South Dakota.

416. On the recommendation of a U.S. government geography board, the "h" at the end of Pittsburgh was dropped in 1890. Public outcry brought back the missing "h" in 1911.

417. More than 150 million cans of SpaghettiOs are consumed each year.

418. The U.S. Central Intelligence Agency (CIA) has its own U.S. Postal ZIP code.

419. The northern Canadian town Flin Flon was named for a character in a paperback science fiction novel.

420. German Daniel Fahrenheit invented the mercury thermometer and his eponymous temperature-measuring scale in the mid-18th century.

421. Cocaine was marketed as a defense against flatulence in the 19th century.

422. A man named Harold Harefoot, whose second name was given to him because of his foot speed and skill at hunting, was King of England from 1037 to

1040.

423. Joseph Kennedy, patriarch of the famed political Kennedy family, was made president of the Columbia Trust Bank at the age of 25.

424. The real Chef Boyardee (Boiardi) was the head chef at the Plaza Hotel in New York City in the 1910s.

425. Mandarin Chinese is the most commonly spoken language on earth.

426. The national flag of Libya consists of only one color: green.

427. There are over 63 million miles of roadway in the world.

428. At the Vetins-Arena football stadium in Germany, beer is distributed to fans via a 5 km-long pipeline running beneath the stadium.

429. The *London Times* was the first-ever newspaper to use the word "Times" as a part of its name.

430. Aluminum is the most common metal in the earth's crust.

431. An ant will normally travel a maximum of approximately 700 feet from its nest.

432. Aristotle's father, Nicomachus, was the personal physician to the King of Macedon.

433. About 160,000 baseballs are used in a Major League Baseball season.

434. An estimated 50 to 70 million people died as a result of World War II.

435. Honey bees ingest and regurgitate nectar numerous times during the production of honey.

436. Airline pilots are not allowed to grow beards.

437. There is no minimum legal drinking age in Cambodia, Albania, Armenia or Norway.

438. The average annual temperature at Dallol, Ethiopia, recorded from 1960-1966, was 34 C/94 F.

439. New Jersey resident and anarchist Gaetano Bresci, angered at Italy's King Umberto I, traveled to Italy, where he shot and killed the king with a revolver in 1900.

440. Kazakhstan is the world's largest completely

landlocked nation.

441. There is no proof that Marie Antoinette ever said "Let them eat cake" during the French Revolution.

442. Iceland has a military force of 130 soldiers.

443. The 72 miles of Interstate 80 between Grand Island and Lincoln, Nebraska is the longest stretch of straight interstate highway in the United States.

444. 7-Up soda was originally known as "Bib-Label Lithiated Lemon-Lime Soda."

445. The word "fart" is one of the oldest words in the English language.

446. One of the main exports of the African nation of Lesotho is water, millions of dollars' worth of which is sold to the nation of South Africa, which completely surrounds the country.

447. Vietnamese revolutionary Ho Chih Minh worked as a baker at the Parker House Hotel in Boston, Massachusetts in 1912-13.

448. Wolfgang Amadeus Mozart began composing music at the age of five.

449. Other than a number of religious texts, Charles Dickens' *A Tale of Two Cities*, at over 200 million copies sold, is believed to be the best-selling book of all time.

450. Boxer Johnny Dundee was knocked out only twice in 330 professional fights during his 30-year fighting career.

451. Future Missouri Senator Thomas Hart Benton shot and wounded future U.S. President Andrew Jackson during a brawl in Nashville, in 1813.

452. Soft-serve ice cream was first sold by Dairy Queen co-founders "Grandpa" and Alex McCullough in Kankakee, Illinois, in 1938.

453. There are 54 sovereign nations on the continent of Africa.

454. Underarm odor is not caused by sweat, but rather by the fermentation of bacteria gathered there.

455. Over 40 million copies of the video game *Super Mario Bros.* have been sold.

456. Commercial citric acid is manufactured from a mold often grown in molasses or corn starch.

457. The deepest man-made hole in the Earth is the

40,266 foot deep Kola Superdeep Borehole in Russia.

458. A pro soccer team in Madagascar won a match 149-0 in 2002 without ever scoring a goal themselves. Members of the opposing team had been told to score at will against themselves as an act of protest.

459. Monrovia, Liberia, named for U.S. President James Monroe, is the only foreign capital named for a U.S. President.

460. Montreal's Ile Notre-Dame is a man-made island built from rock excavated in the construction of the Montreal subway system.

461. Ford's Theatre, the site of the assassination of President Abraham Lincoln, was seized by the U.S. government following the assassination. Its owner, John Ford, was eventually paid $100,000 for the loss of his business.

462. Soy sauce was invented as a way to stretch the use of salt, a rare and valuable commodity at the time.

463. Terrence Malick, Bill Bradley, Robert Penn Warren, Rachel Maddow and Kris Kristofferson were all Rhodes Scholars.

464. Air Force pilot Joseph Kittinger jumped from a plane at 102,800 feet in an experiment for the Air

Force in 1960, reaching a top speed of 614 miles per hour during his descent.

465. Elvis Presley's manager, Colonel Tom Parker, was an illegal immigrant from the Netherlands.

466. The city of Los Angeles began as a small town named "El Pueblo de Nuestra Senora la Reina de los Angeles del Rio de Porciuncula."

467. The first submarines were powered by humans rowing oars.

468. An eagle is depicted on the coat of arms of over 25 nations.

469. There are more than 148,000 hotel rooms in Las Vegas.

470. Killer Whales are known to be loyal to, and swim with, an established extended family that often has its own hunting techniques, as well as unique communication systems.

471. Americans ate approximately 27 billion pounds of beef in 2010.

472. The Mayans were known to smoke cigarettes as far back as the 9th century.

473. Benjamin Franklin invented the lightning rod in 1749.

474. The first person killed by the James gang was a student at William Jewell College, an institution founded in part by Jesse and Frank James' father, Robert James.

475. Fu Manchu, in his original incarnation as a fictional character in a series of Sax Rohmer novels, did not have the mustache that now bears his name, or, for that matter, any facial hair at all.

476. China's Danyang-Kunchan Grand Bridge, spanning 102 miles, is the world's longest bridge.

477. Future U.S. President Jimmy Carter reported seeing a UFO in Leary, Georgia, in 1969.

478. In the original version of *Pinocchio*, the title character is hanged.

479. Pharmacist Eli Lilly, namesake of the massive pharmaceutical company, was a pioneer in using gelatin capsules and fruit-flavored medicine syrups.

480. Historians believe that horned helmets were never used by Vikings in battle.

481. American sign language and British sign

language are completely different, and largely unintelligible by practitioners of the other.

482. German Karl Benz, of Mercedes-Benz fame, invented the gas-powered automobile in the 1870s.

483. Italian volcano Mount Stromboli has been in a state of constant eruption for over 20,000 years.

484. None of the members of the Ramones actually had the surname Ramone.

485. A horse traveling from Mexico to the United States is legally required to spend three days in quarantine.

486. U.N. headquarters in New York City is officially considered an international territory.

487. German pharmacist Julius Neubronner used homing pigeons to deliver medications to his customers in Germany in the early 20th century.

488. Socrates was tried and condemned to death by a jury of 501 Athenian citizens.

489. The Sahara Desert covers more than 3.5 million square miles, roughly the total land area of the entire United States.

490. The first air conditioned cars were introduced by Packard Motors in 1939.

491. The first military air assault in history took place in Venice, Italy, in 1849, when Austrian forces sent unmanned balloons armed with time bombs over the city.

492. Bestselling author Ambrose Bierce traveled to Mexico to cover the Mexican Revolution in 1913. Bierce never returned, and it is unknown to this day what happened to him.

493. Grace Kelly's father, Jack, won three Olympic gold medals in rowing.

494. While performing as a gladiator, the Roman Emperor Claudius fought and defeated a whale.

495. About four million babies are born in the United States each year.

496. Unlike almost all of the other species of cockroach, which are repelled by light, the Asian cockroach is attracted to it.

497. The oldest university in the Americas is the Universidad Michoacana de San Nicolad de Hidalgo in Morelia, Mexico, founded in 1540.

498. The oldest man on record to father a child was 93 years old.

499. Manfred von Richtjhofen, also known as the "Red Baron," was credited with 80 air victories during WWI.

500. The 150,000-seat May Day Stadium in Pyongyang, North Korea, is the world's largest-capacity sports stadium.

501. There are more than 98 million cattle living in the United States.

502. American Naval hero Oliver Hazard Perry was a direct descendant of Scottish hero William Wallace.

503. Citizens of the Czech Republic consume more beer per capita than the people of any other nation in the world.

504. Spaniard Andres De Urdaneta led the second expedition to circumnavigate the world. The successful voyage took nine years to complete.

505. Godzilla has a star on the Hollywood Walk of Fame.

506. All U.S. Medal of Honor recipients are issued standing invitations to U.S. presidential

inaugurations.

507. The northernmost city with over a million residents is St. Petersburg, Russia.

508. The creme filling in the original Oreo cookies was made from lard.

509. The New York Subway system provides an average of five million rides each weekday.

510. Before refrigeration became common, mustard seed was ground together with flour and spices and rolled into dry balls. Consumers mixed these "mustard balls" with a liquid such as wine or vinegar to make a mustard paste.

511. A riot which killed over 90 people in Oxford, England, in 1355, began after two university students got into an altercation with a local tavern owner about the quality of drinks in his establishment.

512. American Eddie Eagan won gold medals in both the summer and winter Olympics, for boxing in 1920 and bobsledding in 1932.

513. The average diameter of the Earth is about 8,000 miles.

514. Guacamole was eaten by the Aztecs as early as

the 1500s.

515. 15 of the 16 largest high school basketball gymnasiums in the U.S. are located in the state of Indiana.

516. More than seven billion cans of Spam have been sold by Hormel Foods Corporation since it introduced the processed meat product in 1937.

517. A majority of Bonobo monkeys are bisexual.

518. The English channel separates England and France by only 21 miles at its narrowest point.

519. Charles Shulz published 17,897 Peanuts comic strips during his career.

520. Famed politician George Clinton was the governor of New York for 22 years.

521. The Rocket Frog can jump up to 40 times its own body length.

522. The United States government spent 3.518 billion dollars in 2009.

523. The smallest dinosaurs known to have existed were around the size of a pigeon.

524. 1,517 of the total 2,223 passengers of the Titanic lost their lives in the 1912 sinking.

525. There are more than nine million people living in prisons around the world.

526. The brewery at Weihenstephan Abbey in Germany has been brewing beer since 1040. It is the longest continually-operating brewery in the world.

527. Television host and Johnny Carson sidekick Ed McMahon worked as, among other things, a bingo caller and a carnival barker before hitting it big in Hollywood.

528. Carrier pigeons can cover up to 99 miles in one round trip.

529. The average annual daily high temperature in Reykjavik, Iceland, is 7 C/44.6 F.

530. Some ancient Chinese believed that an animal leaping over a corpse would lead to the deceased becoming a zombie.

531. The annual crime rate in the U.S. is believed to have escalated as much as 25% upon the enforcement of Prohibition in 1920.

532. The numerically lowest postal ZIP code in the

United States is 00501, which represents a part of Holtsville, New York.

533. The world's first passenger railway connected Liverpool and Manchester, England, in 1830.

534. Physician Samuel Mudd, who set John Wilkes Booth's broken leg following the assassination of President Abraham Lincoln, was sentenced to life in prison in 1865. Mudd was pardoned and released four years later by Lincoln's successor, Andrew Johnson.

535. Professional baseball player Old Hoss Radbourn, in an 1886 Boston Beaneater team photo, is shown extending his middle finger towards the camera. The gesture is believed to be the first recorded instance of someone "flipping the bird."

536. Hand grenades were widely used in the U.S. Civil War.

537. The world's first self-serve grocery store was the Piggly Wiggly store, opened in Memphis in 1916.

538. The official motto of Sussex County, England is "We wunt be druv."

539. The liberal and conservative political views known as "left wing" and "right wing" date back to the French Revolution, when supporters of the two

sides gathered at opposite sides, or "wings," of the National Assembly.

540. An estimated 36 million people live in Tokyo and its surrounding suburban area.

541. The top speed ever attained by an unmanned railed vehicle was 6,462 miles per hour.

542. In the 1870s, some 700,000 head of cattle were herded from Texas to the cow town of Abilene, Kansas, each year.

543. Only two African nations, Ethiopia and Liberia, were never colonized by European nations.

544. An Adjunct bird of Asia and Africa stands about 5 feet tall.

545. An average male Bengal tiger weighs nearly 500 pounds.

546. The first night game of the NFL was played in Rhode Island on November 6, 1929. The Chicago Cardinals defeated the Providence Steam Roller.

547. The ancient Lydians used entire battalions of fighting dogs during military campaigns.

548. John Adams was admitted to Harvard College at the age of 16.

549. Weasels and ferrets often perform a "weasel war dance," a serious of hops and hisses, after winning a fight or succeeding in securing food from competitors.

550. The father of Sex Pistols' bassist Sid Vicious worked as a guard at Buckingham Palace.

551. The waters of Venezuela's Angel Falls drop 2,648 feet.

552. William Penn, William Wallace, Samuel Pepys, Rudolf Hess, Sir Walter Raleigh and Queen Elizabeth I were all held as prisoners in the Tower of London.

553. The actual position of the equator on earth drifts up to 30 feet every year.

554. The first computer mouse was built by Douglas Engelbart at the Stanford Research Institute in 1963.

555. The gunfight at the O.K. Corral is believed to have lasted about 30 seconds.

556. Slugs have both male and female reproductive organs.

557. There are over 33,000 Subway restaurants around the world.

558. 60% of the land used for agriculture in Greece is dedicated to the production of olives.

559. Snatiation is the scientific word for the phenomenon of sneezing fits caused by a full stomach.

560. Scotland's Elaine Davidson has over 6,000 body piercings.

561. Over 100 people were killed when soldiers opened fire on a group of citizens rioting over the increased price of bread in Milan, Italy, in 1898.

562. An estimated 142 billion dollars worth of marijuana is sold around the world every year.

563. Lawyers do not have to pass a bar examination to practice law in Mexico, they only have to hold a law degree.

564. In 1994, Michael Crichton produced the #1 rated television show, *ER*, wrote the novel and screenplay for the #1 movie *Jurassic Park* and had the #1 book on the *New York Times* bestseller list with *Disclosure*.

565. Dolly Madison's sister, Lucy, was married to

George Washington's nephew, who was also named George Washington.

566. The U.S. state with the most counties is Texas with 254. Delaware, with three, has the least.

567. Jim Beam Whiskey was originally called Old Jake Beam Whiskey.

568. The Democratic Republic of the Congo is the world's most populous officially French-speaking nation.

569. The highest wind speed ever recorded was a gust of 484 kmh/301 mph near Oklahoma City, Oklahoma in 1999.

570. The average life-span of a Monarch butterfly is two months.

571. The Mongol Empire of the 13th and 14th centuries was the world's largest contiguous empire ever, covering almost 13 million square miles at the height of its power.

572. The Arctic Tern, a seabird, flies over 44,000 miles a year as it migrates between the Arctic Circle and Antarctica.

573. Monosodium glutamate is produced from the

fermentation of bacteria or yeast.

574. There are over two million asteroids orbiting the sun in the "asteroid belt" located between Mars and Jupiter.

575. Painter Pablo Picasso's birth name was "Pablo Diego José Francisco de Paula Juan Nepomuceno María de los Remedios Crispiniano de la Santísima Trinidad."

576. In even-numbered years, the months of February, March and November start on the same day of the week.

577. The November 1972 edition of *Playboy* magazine sold 7,161,561 copies, the most for any issue of the magazine.

578. Seven U.S. states: Alabama, Alaska, Hawaii, Mississippi, Nevada, Utah and Wyoming have no state lottery.

579. Japanese people have the world's longest life expectancy: 82.6 years.

580. The practice of shaving began in ancient times as a defense against enemies grabbing and pulling soldiers by their beards during battle.

581. Over five trillion cigarettes are smoked each year worldwide.

582. Tennessee Williams was born in Mississippi and grew up in Missouri. He never lived in Tennessee.

583. A giant "honey mushroom" in the Malheur National Forest of Oregon occupies an area of over 2,200 acres.

584. The New York Police Department employs around 40,000 people.

585. An estimated one million people died while building the Great Wall of China.

586. The movie *Tron* was partly inspired by the early video game Pong.

587. There is enough concrete in Hoover Dam to pave a highway from coast to coast across the United States.

588. Jackie Robinson, before his Major League career, became the athletics director at Samuel Huston College in Austin, Texas, at the age of 25.

589. The world's first cellular phone weighed about 2-1/2 pounds.

590. Ethiopian Haile Gebrselassie ran at an average speed of 12.6 miles per hour for 26 miles and 385 yards when he set the record time for running a marathon in 2008.

591. Explorer James Cook was killed in Hawaii in 1779, after attempting to take the King of Hawaii hostage in order to exchange him for a stolen boat.

592. People have been playing Tic-Tac-Toe since the first century BC.

593. England's famed Sherwood Forest has been reduced to a mere 1.63 square mile wooded area.

594. The AMF chain of bowling centers traces its roots to Rufus L. Patterson, who was the inventor of the automated cigarette vending machine.

595. Model T Fords were assembled at factories in the United States, Japan, Argentina, Canada, England, Spain, Denmark, France, Belgium, Brazil and Norway during the early 20th century.

596. The habanero chili pepper originated in Cuba; the word "habanero" means "from Havana" in Spanish.

597. The most popular dog breed in the U.S. is the Labrador Retriever.

598. The first college fraternity was the Phi Beta Kappa Society, which was chartered at William and Mary College in Virginia, in 1776.

599. France's Palace of Versailles has 700 rooms and over 2,100 windows.

600. The first distillery established in America began operations in 1640 in what is now New York City.

601. The Alabama state capital building served as the capital of the Confederate States of America for three months before being relocated to Richmond, Virginia.

602. At the height of its power, the Mongol Empire controlled over 21 million square miles.

603. There are an estimated 1.4 billion lightning flashes around the world each year.

604. The Beastie Boys are often credited with coining the term "Mullet" to describe the hairstyle of short on top and long in the back.

605. The city of King of Prussia, Pennsylvania, took its name from a tavern located in the area known as the King of Prussia Inn.

606. Chess legend Bobby Fischer and musical artists Barbara Streisand and Neil Diamond were all

schoolmates at Brooklyn's Erasmus Hall High School during the 1950s.

607. Salt is a common ingredient in soft drinks.

608. The first 3D movie shown to a paying public audience was *The Power of Love*, which was shown in Los Angeles in 1922.

609. A U.S. state, an Indian tribe, a river and a bay were all named for English nobleman Thomas West the Baron De La Warr (Delaware).

610. Due to heat-sensitive chemical components, a Siamese cat's hair is white in warmer parts of the body and darker in the cooler parts like the feet, lower legs and face.

611. Five U.S. states: Alaska, Arizona, Hawaii, New Mexico and Oklahoma, were admitted to the Union in the 20th century.

612. Swedish Surstromming, also known as Scandinavian Rotten Fish, is a fermented, canned herring foodstuff that scientist have found to be the worst-smelling food in the world.

613. Early traffic lights included an audible buzzer to notify the motorist that the light was about to change.

614. John Wilkes Booth organized an unsuccessful kidnapping attempt on President Abraham Lincoln in March of 1865.

615. Radar specialist Jacob Beser was the only man to fly on both the Hiroshima and Nagasaki atomic bombings in 1945.

616. The oldest person to win an Olympic gold medal was Sweden's Oscar Swahn, at the age of 72, won gold in a shooting event in the 1920 summer games.

617. Neil Armstrong walked approximately 65 feet away from his landing craft during the first moon landing in 1969.

618. Riots broke out in Malawi in 2003 when citizens claimed that there had been a large number of vampire attacks in the country.

619. A Bald Eagle's nest can weigh over a ton.

620. Banker and industrialist J.P. Morgan owned parts of 42 different corporations during his business career.

621. The saxophone was invented by Belgian Adolphe Sax in 1914.

622. While sitting in his Dallas home in 1963, U.S.

Army General Edwin Walker was shot and wounded by Lee Harvey Oswald, only seven months before the assassination of John F. Kennedy.

623. Edgar Allan Poe's first published work, a book of poetry, was written under the pen name "A Bostonian."

624. The Roman ruler Marc Antony was believed to have been the modern equivalent of five million dollars in debt by the age of 20.

625. The NHL's New Jersey Devils are named for a legendary flying creature that is said to inhabit the Pine Barrens section of southern New Jersey.

626. Although Santiago is the capital city of Chile, the Chilean legislature meets in the city of Valparaiso.

627. In the United States, more babies are born on Wednesday than any other day of the week.

628. Somewhere between eight and 11 million Russian soldiers died during World War II.

629. Cockroach tea is used as a medicinal remedy in some parts of the world.

630. The world's first hand grenades, ceramic jars

filled with a napalm-like flaming substance, were used in combat as early as the 8th century.

631. Approximately 33,000 people live in the 808,000 square miles of the Canadian province of Nunavut.

632. Beer was a gift commonly given to ancient Egyptian Pharaohs.

633. Raytheon engineer Percy Spencer discovered the concept behind the microwave oven when he accidentally melted a chocolate bar while working with radar equipment in 1945.

634. General Motors sold over eight million vehicles in 2008.

635. The boreal forest, or taiga, a vast forest that covers the northern parts of Asia and North America, contains almost a third of the world's trees.

636. Sideburns were named after U.S. Civil War General Ambrose Burnside, who wore long sideburns that connected directly with a mustache and a clean-shaven chin.

637. Marcel Proust's novel in seven parts, *In Remembrance of Things Past*, is approximately 1.5 million words long.

638. The Hindenberg made 17 successful commercial transatlantic flights before famously crashing in New Jersey in 1937.

639. Reed Hastings, one of the founders of Netflix, got the idea to start the video rental company after being charged a late fee on a rental of the movie *Apollo 13*.

640. In 16 years of leadership, Alexander the Great was never defeated in battle.

641. There are .067 people per square mile in Greenland, and 16,444 per square mile in Hong Kong.

642. Both the Philadelphia Athletics and Cincinnati Reds passed on deals to acquire Babe Ruth before he went to the Red Sox in 1914.

643. The Native American city of Cahokia, in Illinois, just across the Mississippi River from modern-day St. Louis, was the most populous city in what is now the United States until it was surpassed by Philadelphia in 1800.

644. Before 1994, Doritos tortilla chips had pointed, rather than rounded, corners.

645. Lima, Peru is home to the world's first one-way

street.

646. Tchaikovsky's score for the fam
Overture calls for the firing of 16 can

647. Actress and entertainer Mae West was the second-highest paid person in the United States in 1935, just behind newspaper mogul William Randolph Hearst.

648. The first cucumber pickles sold packed in glass jars were introduced by the father and son team of Frank and Joe Vlasic in Detroit in 1942.

649. The original Superman was created as a villain bent on world domination. The character was later changed to a hero by creators Jerry Siegel and Joe Shuster.

650. King Umberto I of Italy survived two assassination attempts before succumbing to four bullets from an anarchist in 1900.

651. The simple declaration "I marry you" was all that was required to officially become married in the Middle Ages.

652. Johnny Appleseed, whose real name was John Chapman, would return periodically to the apple nurseries that he had planted to collect the profits

.ed from fruit sales.

653. Certain owls use a snake-like hissing noise to scare away enemies.

654. Joseph Conrad, who wrote, in English, classics such as *Lord Jim*, *Nostromo* and *Heart of Darkness*, did not speak the language until he was in his twenties.

655. Coyotes are not known to attack or eat roadrunners.

656. Over 200,000 people are arrested for drunk driving in California each year.

657. Louis XIV became the King of France at the age of four.

658. During his famous "march to the sea," William Tecumseh Sherman used census data in order to plan a route through confederate Georgia which would contain the most goods and farms to pillage for his army.

659. The first auto manufacturer to include safety belts as a standard feature was Saab in 1958.

660. James Spangler, a janitor whose asthma was irritated when sweeping dust, invented the first

upright vacuum in 1908.

661. As young men, Bill Clinton and Steven Spielberg worked together on the presidential election campaign of George McGovern.

662. The grey fox and the raccoon dog are the only canines known to have the ability to climb trees.

663. Due to its German origin, sauerkraut was officially known as "Liberty Cabbage" in the U.S. during World War I.

664. The letter "A" was adapted from an Egyptian hieroglyphic symbol shaped like an ox.

665. Tim Mara bought the NFL's New York Giants for $500 in 1925.

666. Motley Crue's 1989 hit single "Kickstart my Heart" was inspired by band member Nikki Sixx's 1987 overdose and subsequent revival by two adrenaline shots to the heart.

667. Frenchman Louis-Sebastien Lenormand made the world's first successful parachute jump in 1783, when he completed a jump from a building in his hometown of Montpelier.

668. The *Guinness Book of World Records* originated

as the result of an argument over what game bird of Europe was the fastest.

669. The first menthol cigarette, the Spud, was introduced in 1924.

670. Many early baseball bats were flat.

671. Frances Cleveland, wife of Grover Cleveland, became the youngest first lady in the history of the United States when she married the president at the age of 21, in 1886.

672. Because of the great height of Venezuela's Angel Falls, much of the water falling from its crest evaporates before reaching the base of the falls.

673. Writer James Joyce, due to a childhood dog attack, was terrified of dogs.

674. The modern calendar system, developed and put into official use in 1582, is called the Gregorian Calendar in honor of Pope Gregory XIII.

675. The world's first general interest magazine, *The Gentleman's Magazine*, was published in England beginning in 1731.

676. The largest St. Bernard on record weighed 220 pounds.

677. Lord Baltimore, despite never setting foot in America, governed the colony of Maryland for 42 years.

678. The origin of "peeping Tom" comes from the Lady Godiva legend. Tom was said to have been struck blind when he snuck a peek as the nude Lady Godiva rode through town.

679. Pakistan's Allama Iqbal Open University is the world's largest university, with an enrollment of over 1.8 million students.

680. 26 of the 44 U.S. presidents have been lawyers.

681. Loving County, Texas, is the only county in the United States with no one living under the poverty line.

682. With a wingspan of up to one foot, the Queen Alexandra's Birdswing is the largest butterfly in the world.

683. An estimated 40 million people lost their lives due to Mongol invasions led by Genghis Khan.

684. Paul Newman's food company, Newman's Own, has donated over 300 million dollars to charity.

685. The game of chess traces its origin back to 6th

century India.

686. Rapper and hype man Flavor Flav is proficient at over a dozen musical instruments.

687. Arthur Conan Doyle's famous character Sherlock Holmes was killed in an 1893 short story. After a huge public outcry, Doyle brought the character back in the 1901 novel *The Hound of the Baskervilles*.

688. North American Indians were brewing beer years before the arrival of any Europeans on the continent.

689. The first mobile phone call from a vehicle took place in St. Louis in 1946. The equipment used to place the call weighed 80 pounds.

690. Kool-Aid was once available in chocolate flavor.

691. Canada's Highway 401, near Toronto, is North America's busiest highway, with an estimated 400,000-plus vehicles traveling on it each day.

692. There are over 8,500 Wal Mart stores in the world.

693. Scientist Marie Curie the first woman to win a Nobel Prize and the first person to win two Nobel

Prizes.

694. A skunk can spray its smelly fluid up to 16 feet.

695. Irish author and playwright Samuel Beckett was a standout cricket player at Dublin University.

696. Every state in the United States, except Alaska, Hawaii, Louisiana and Oklahoma, has a town named Riverside.

697. Saint George is the patron saint of, among others, England, Georgia, Greece, Portugal, Russia and Lithuania.

698. In New York City in 1854, a woman named Elizabeth Jennings Graham, an African-American, was ejected from a horse-drawn trolley by the driver and a policeman. Graham sued, with the help of lawyer and future U.S. President Chester Arthur, and won, effectively beginning the end of segregation on public transportation in New York City.

699. Legally, a Vidalia onion can only be grown in a specific 20-county area in the U.S. state of Georgia.

700. On average, a Major League baseball player uses around 100 bats in a season.

701. The largest elephant ever measured was over 33

feet long and weighed 24,000 pounds.

702. A violin maker is known as a luthier.

703. A sneeze can project fluids to a distance of up to 20 feet.

704. A female ogre is known as an ogress.

705. Millions of methamphetamine tablets were issued to both Allied and Axis soldiers during World War II.

706. Motion picture mogul Samuel Goldwyn used the last name Goldfish before changing it to the more familiar Goldwyn.

707. In the mid-400s B.C., Greek thinker Anaxagoras became the first person to theorize that the moon and the sun were giant spherical rocks.

708. The most expensive wristwatch ever purchased was bought at an auction in 2010 for 5.5 million dollars.

709. One of the earliest types of time-keeping devices used water draining from a pot to mark time.

710. The modern wooden clothespin was invented by

David Smith of Vermont, in 1853.

711. There are approximately 55,000 miles of crude oil pipelines pumping oil beneath the United States.

712. Moroccan Hicham El Guerrouj ran the mile in a record time of 3.43 minutes in the Grand Prix in Rome, in 1999.

713. The first *Boston Globe* newspaper was published in 1872 and cost four cents to purchase.

714. The Global Positioning System is provided by a group of 30 satellites constantly orbiting the earth.

715. The Bugatti Veyron, the world's fastest road-legal automobile, can reach a top speed of 267 mph.

716. Every barber pole made in the United States is manufactured by the William Marvy Company of St. Paul, Minnesota.

717. An average American eats ten pounds of marshmallows each year.

718. Jiuquan, China, is the largest "city" by area in the world, encompassing almost 65,000 square miles.

719. The average age of a U.S. president at the time

of his taking office is 54 years.

720. Before foul poles came into use, some Major League ballparks used ropes strung from the foul line to the back of the bleachers to determine if a home run was fair or foul.

721. Vladimir Lenin's brother Aleksander, was arrested and executed in 1887 after an assassination attempt against Tsar Alexander III.

722. On October 28, 1919, U.S. President Woodrow Wilson vetoed the "Volstead Act" which outlawed alcohol. It was reinstated by the U.S. Congress a day later.

723. The indigenous name for Africa's Victoria Falls is Mosi-oa-Tunay, which translates to "smoke that thunders."

724. Aluminum was once more valuable than gold.

725. The first Sears, Roebuck and Company catalog featured only watches.

726. The towns of Ringling, Montana and Ringling, Oklahoma, were named in honor of circus impresario John Ringling.

727. Most consumer vegetable oil is made from

rapeseed.

728. What is considered the world's first successful helicopter flight took place in France in 1907, when the pilot was lifted one foot off of the ground for a duration of 20 seconds.

729. *Playboy* magazine was originally slated to be titled *Stag Party*.

730. Paul Tibbets, the pilot of the Enola Gay, the bomber which dropped the atom bomb on Hiroshima, was often employed as the personal pilot for General Dwight Eisenhower during World War II.

731. Every American G.I. was issued a weekly ration of cigarettes during World War II.

732. Excessive consumption of licorice or licorice candy can lead to multiple health problems, including high blood pressure, headaches and muscle weakness.

733. Golfer Mike Austin hammered a record 515 yard drive during a senior tournament in Las Vegas in 1974.

734. A Spanish ban on the growing of sideburns by the indigenous people of Mexico caused a series of riots in the late 17th century.

735. Jimmy Carter has published more books (24) than any other U.S. president.

736. Key West, Florida, is closer to Havana, Cuba (106 miles), than it is to Miami (129 miles).

737. The name of the Adirondack Mountains is descended from a Mohawk Indian phrase meaning "they eat trees."

738. Scissors are believed to have been in use beginning in Egypt, around 1500 BC.

739. A Russian woman, whose first name is unknown but who was married to a man named Feodor Vassilyev, is said to have given birth to 69 children, including 16 sets of twins, seven sets of triplets and four sets of quadruplets.

740. At 16,732 feet above sea level, the town of La Rinconada, Peru, is the world's highest permanent settlement.

741. Over 1.5 million people graduate from college each year in the United States.

742. Soldiers who fought in the American Civil War were paid $11 to $16 per month for their service.

743. There is no specific scientific term for

"boogers." They are often referred to as "dried nasal mucus."

744. Egypt's Great Pyramid of Giza was the world's tallest man-made object for a period of 3,800 years.

745. A single shrimp can lay up to one million eggs at once.

746. Both Winston Churchill and Princess Diana were descendants of the aristocratic Spencer family of Great Britain.

747. In the 1930s, New Englander W.G. Peacock combined beet, celery, carrot, lettuce, parsley, watercress, spinach and tomato juice into a popular juice drink which later became known as V-8.

748. The Eastern European "nation" of Transnistria, while not being recognized as an independent nation by any outside governing body, declared its independence in 1990 and operates its own presidential government, military, postal service, police force and currency system.

749. Charles Lindbergh was awarded the Medal of Honor for his 1927 transatlantic flight.

750. Pictures of five different women were found in Lincoln assassin John Wilkes Booth's pocket after he

was killed in a raid 12 days after the assassination.

751. When attacked, an aardvark will roll onto its back and defend itself with its claws.

752. The Berretta company of Italy began manufacturing firearms in the year 1526.

753. In some cultures a male "unibrow" is considered a sign of manliness.

754. Dogs often yawn when confused.

755. It rains an average of 200 days a year in Brussels, Belgium.

756. The Van Camp company began as a supplier of canned pork and beans to the Union army during the U.S. Civil War.

757. The slugburger, a deep fried patty made of meat and soy grits or flour and egg, which was originally served during lean times during World War II, is still popular in restaurants in northeastern Mississippi.

758. Because it was built on the soft floor of a drained lake, the city of Mexico City is continuously sinking.

759. HBO founder Charles Dolan set up the first

underground cable television system in Manhattan in 1965.

760. The artificial sweetener saccharin was first produced in 1878.

761. The Bolas spider uses a long string of silk with a sticky blob at the end to swing at, and catch, passing moths.

762. A three-toed sloth can reach a top speed of 0.15 miles per hour.

763. Lanolin, a substance used in many products such as lip balms and cosmetics, is a wax excreted by sheep.

764. Baseball Hall of Famers Eddie Murray and Ozzie Smith were teammates at Los Angeles' Locke High School.

765. Only eight of the 44 U.S. presidents were born west of the Mississippi River.

766. Twinkies were originally filled with banana flavored creme.

767. Mongol invaders used an early form of biological warfare, when they employed catapults to fling cadavers infected with the Black Death plague

into the besieged Crimean city of Caffa in the 14th century.

768. A man named Jay Stokes completed a record 640 sky diving jumps in one day.

769. The European equivalent of the American "Boogeyman" is the "Sackman" who carries away children in a large cloth sack.

770. In 1910-11, French grape growers, facing tough economic times and controversies over rights to the name "Champagne," rioted and burned buildings. The French government was forced to call out 40,000 troops to quell what became known as the "Champagne Riots."

771. A lost eyelash takes seven to eight weeks to regrow.

772. The highest recorded temperature in history was 57.8 C/136 F, in Al'aziziyah, Libya, in 1922.

773. The first public cellular phone call was made by Motorola executive Martin Cooper in New York City in 1973.

774. One in every five persons in the world is Chinese.

775. There are over 48,000 miles of interstate highway in the United States.

776. There are 255,168 different ways in which a game of Tic-Tac-Toe can play out.

777. Over 1.8 million gallons of beer are consumed during the annual Oktoberfest celebration in Munich, Germany each year.

778. The slot machine was invented in San Francisco by a man named Charles Fey in the 1880s.

779. A Bengal tiger's roar can be heard from almost two miles away.

780. Napoleon Bonaparte was terrified of cats.

781. Australian Lawrence Bragg, who, along with his father, was awarded the Nobel Prize for Physics in 1915, is the youngest person (age 25) to win a Nobel prize.

782. The world's first miniature golf course was constructed in 1867 in St. Andrews, Scotland. St. Andrews is also home to one of the oldest golf courses in the world, the Royal and Ancient of St. Andrews, founded in 1754.

783. The recliner, later dubbed the La-Z-Boy, was

invented by cousins Edwin Shoemaker and Edwin Knabusch in Monroe, Michigan, in 1928.

784. Western legend Wyatt Earp often earned extra money as a boxing referee.

785. The Valdosta Wildcats of Georgia are the winningest high school football program in history. The Wildcats have won over 860 games and maintained a .780 winning percentage.

786. The facial-hair combination of a goatee and a mustache is called a Van Dyke, in honor of the 17th century Flemish painter Anthony van Dyck, who helped popularize the style.

787. In Caribbean legend, a mythological female vampire, called the Loogaroo, hunts for the blood of humans. Tradition has it that she will compulsively count grains of sand or rice on the ground; so, as garlic is used to protect people from the European vampire, piles of sand and rice are used to fend off the Loogaroo.

788. Due to the quinine in tonic water, the liquid will glow bright blue when put under a black light.

789. The first Apple computer, the Apple I, entered the market in 1976 and could be purchased for the price of $666.66.

790. John Wilkes Booth was in the crowd at President Abraham Lincoln's second inauguration in 1865.

791. About $9 billion worth of diamonds are mined each year.

792. Mahatma Gandhi was married at the age of 13.

793. An estimated 2 million people from outside Tokyo enter and leave the city for work or other reasons each day.

794. At the height of production in 1914, the Ford Motor Company could assemble a Model T in around 93 minutes.

795. Theodore Geisel assumed his pen name, Dr. Seuss, in order to continue writing for the school magazine at Dartmouth after he was caught drinking gin on campus.

796. The Braille system traces its roots to Napoleon's desire for a communication system that could be utilized in total darkness.

797. A chigger is approximately 0.4 millimeters in length.

798. Martin Ignacio de Loyola was the first person to circumnavigate the world twice. He did it once in

each direction.

799. During World War I, Germany became the first nation in the world to use Daylight Saving Time.

800. The U.S. Library of Congress contains over 32 million books.

801. There are an estimated five million animal species yet to be officially identified.

802. Before entering politics, Lyndon B. Johnson was a school teacher in Texas.

803. All of the counties in Kansas are, by default, "dry". Individual county governments must choose to allow liquor sales.

804. New York City's first subway opened in 1904 and ran from Manhattan to the Bronx.

805. Abraham Lincoln was assassinated only four days after the surrender of Robert E. Lee at Appomattox Court House in Virginia.

806. Fermented urine, called Lant, was used by the ancient Romans as a cleaning agent.

807. The ratcheting socket wrench was invented in

Vermont by J.J. Richardson in 1863.

808. Honeydew honey is made by bees who ingest the secretions of sap-sucking insects.

809. British Air Force pilot Andy Green drove a rocket-propelled wheeled vehicle at a speed of 714.144 miles per hour in 1997, setting the world land speed record.

810. Many state and local road maintenance crews spray beet juice onto roads and highways to help melt ice during the winter.

811. Snakes kill an estimated 94,000 humans each year.

812. In the Pittsburgh, Pennsylvania, area many people refer to bologna as "jumbo".

813. The main function of the eyebrow is to prevent moisture, such as sweat, from flowing into the eye.

814. In some places, cow manure is used to line the floors and walls of buildings as a natural insect repellant.

815. The earliest European explorers to reach what is now New Zealand believed that the island was located just to the south of the continent of South

America.

816. Dr. James Salisbury, a New York physician who believed good health could be improved be increasing meat intake and limiting vegetables, originated the Salisbury Steak in 1888. Dr. Salisbury recommended that the steaks be consumed three times each day.

817. In the late 19th century, cocaine, complete with a needle for injection, could be openly purchased at drug stores in the United States.

818. The president of the United States receives an annual salary of $400,000.

819. Viking Erik the Red set up his settlement in Greenland after killing a "number of men" during a feud in Iceland in the year 982.

820. The Duncan Hines company traces its roots to a food rating guidebook published by the company's namesake, Duncan Hines, who worked as a traveling salesman in the 1930s.

821. Over 21,000 people died during the initial, and failed, French attempt at constructing the Panama Canal in the 1880s.

822. The first postage stamps were introduced in the United Kingdom in 1840.

823. The Philippines was named for King Philip II of Spain.

824. The geographic center of the United States is about 20 miles north of Belle Fourche, South Dakota.

825. Satellites no longer in use are often moved to a "graveyard orbit" where they orbit with other non-operational satellites.

826. President Harry Truman was both the lowest-ever and highest-ever rated president in terms of public approval during his tenure as president.

827. Writer Boris Pasternak was awarded the Nobel Prize for Literature in 1958, but was forced by officials of the Soviet Union to decline the award.

828. The Chase Bank traces its roots to a company founded by Aaron Burr in New York, in 1799.

829. A scrivener was a literate person who charged a fee to read and write documents for the illiterate.

830. Although officially considered citizens of the United States, Puerto Ricans are not allowed to vote in U.S. presidential elections.

831. The temperature in Asia's Gobi Desert has been known to fluctuate up to as much as 35 C/61 F, in a

single 24 hour period.

832. Carousels date back to as early as the year 500 AD.

833. Glasses or globes filled with water were used as magnifiers in ancient Rome.

834. A tarantula can live up to 25 years.

835. Lawyers and the legal profession were barred in France in 1789, but later reinstated.

836. Damascus, Syria is thought to be the oldest continuously inhabited city in the world.

837. The world's largest beaver dam, at over one mile in length, is located in Canada's Wood Buffalo National Park.

838. Water is the island of Fiji's number one export.

839. Boston Corbett, the Union Army private who shot and killed John Wilkes Booth in Virginia in 1865, castrated himself with a pair of scissors in 1858 in order to avoid visiting prostitutes, which was against his religion.

840. The first wristwatch was made by the Patek

Philippe company of Switzerland in 1868.

841. A leopard will eat any animal that it can successfully catch and kill.

842. Since 1876, every University of Arkansas graduate's name has been etched into a concrete sidewalk that now stretches over five miles and contains over 140,000 names.

843. Over 35 billion gallons of beer is drunk annually.

844. Many of the diamonds mined today were formed at the location of ancient meteor strikes.

845. When Hillary Clinton ran for senator of the state of New York in 2000, it marked the first time that a first lady had ever run for public office.

846. Actor Rip Torn attacked author Norman Mailer with a hammer during the filming of Mailer's 1970 movie *Maidstone*.

847. Honduras and El Salvador fought a four day "soccer war" in 1969, after riots which arose from a series of soccer matches between the national teams of each country.

848. The Coors brewing company manufactured

malted milk during Prohibition.

849. Al Capone's nickname was "Scarface." The man who slashed Capone's face with a knife was later hired by the famous criminal as a bodyguard.

850. Urine was used in the manufacture of early forms of gunpowder.

851. The Spanish word "burrito" means "small donkey."

852. During his lifetime, Charles Lindbergh was awarded the U.S. Medal of Honor, the French Legion of Honor, the Royal Air Force Cross from the British, the Distinguished Flying Cross and a Pulitzer Prize.

853. Approximately 85% of the African-American population that was legally eligible to enlist in the Union Army did so during the Civil War.

854. More than 1,200 people have committed suicide by jumping from the Golden Gate Bridge in San Francisco.

855. The first stop sign was placed in the U.S. state of Michigan in 1915.

856. Harriet Tubman is believed to have helped around 350 slaves escape their bondage during her

time with the underground railroad in the 1850s and 1860s.

857. More than 300,000 people climb Japan's Mt. Fuji each year.

858. The Pogo stick was invented in Germany by partners Max Pohling and Ernst Gottschall in 1920; they used the first two letters of their surnames to give the invention its unique name.

859. Over 100 billion dollars is spent on legal gambling in the United States each year.

860. Royal Caribbean's MS Oasis of the Seas cruise ship can accommodate over 6,000 passengers.

861. Hurricane Katrina caused over $81 billion dollars in damages and killed at least 1,800 people.

862. The world's first subway system opened beneath London in 1863.

863. General George Patton died after a car accident that occurred on his way to a pheasant hunting trip in Germany in 1945.

864. Crushed charcoal and stones were sometimes used as tooth powder for brushing teeth in ancient times.

865. In some parts of Africa, mice are seen as a delicacy.

866. A University of Alberta computer program, called Chinook, has been programmed so that it is impossible for an opponent to beat it at checkers; the best outcome to be hoped for is a draw.

867. Gunfighter Doc Holliday turned to gambling in the late 19th century, when he saw a decline in his dentistry practice due to constant coughing brought on by tuberculosis.

868. The first satellite used in GPS navigation was launched in 1989.

869. A record 31.1m/1,224 inches of snow fell on Mount Rainier in Washington in a one-year period in the 1970s.

870. Adolph Coors, the founder of Coors Brewing, leapt to his death from a Virginia Beach, Virginia, hotel in 1929.

871. The first gambling casino in Europe was opened in Venice, Italy, in 1638.

872. The United States-Canada border is the longest national border in the world. The United States-Mexico border is the second longest.

873. The city of Fargo, North Dakota, was named in honor of Wells Fargo founder William Fargo.

874. Parents in ancient Rome could legally sell their children into slavery.

875. Early Americans considered the lobster a food for the poor and often used it as bait.

876. American Wiley Post became the first person to fly solo around the world when he completed the feat in 1933. Post, and passenger Will Rogers, died in a plane crash in Alaska only two years later.

877. Bubble gum is typically pink because that is the only color dye that its inventor, Walter Diemer, had on hand at the time of its creation.

878. Former Cuban leader Fulgencio Batista died of a heart attack in Spain in 1973, only days before a team of assassins sent by Fidel Castro were set to kill him.

879. "Wiff-Waff", the forerunner of table tennis, began as a game in which books were used as paddles to hit a golf ball back and forth on a table.

880. Al Capone was expelled from school at the age of 14 for striking a teacher in the face.

881. The world's first drive-in was opened by A&W

Root Beer co-founder Roy Allen in Sacramento, in 1919.

882. Davy Crockett was a member of the U.S. House of Representatives before raising a volunteer company to fight in Texas, and ultimately the Alamo, where they met their deaths.

883. The longest non-stop airline flight currently in operation is the 9,500 mile, nearly 19-hour flight between Newark, New Jersey and Singapore.

884. An estimated 40% of all marriages end in divorce.

885. The Gila Monster and the Mexican beaded lizard are the only two venomous lizards.

886. The average toll for ships using the Panama Canal is approximately $54,000.

887. Taurine, one of the ingredients of many popular energy drinks, was first found in its natural form in the bile of oxen in the 1820s.

888. The first American military installation in Hawaii was built inside the crater of the Diamond Head Volcano, in 1909.

889. More than 350 million legal border crossings

take place between the United States and Mexico each year.

890. Oscar winning French screenwriter and director Albert Lamorisse invented the board game *Risk* in 1957.

891. Christopher Columbus first set foot in the "New World" on land that is now part of the nation of Honduras.

892. James Joyce worked for seven years on his novel *Ulysses*.

893. Australian citizens over the age of 18 are required, by law, to vote in all federal elections.

894. Robert E. Lee led federal forces in the pursuit and capture of John Brown's anti-slavery group at Harpers Ferry, Virginia, in 1859.

895. Caribou are known to travel over 3,000 miles in a year.

896. There are at least 250,000 words in the English language.

897. Amazon.com was originally slated to be called Cadabra.com. The original name was scrapped because of its similarity to the word "cadaver."

898. Wales-born pirate Bartholomew Roberts is believed to have captured almost 500 vessels during his career as a privateer.

899. Director Steven Spielberg was twice denied admission to the USC film school in the 1960s.

900. Famous ragtime composer and musician Scott Joplin was awarded a Pulitzer Prize in 1972, 55 years after his death.

901. A person jumping from the Golden Gate Bridge enters the water at an estimated 76 miles per hour.

902. Hot air balloons were regularly used for observation and reconnaissance by both sides of the American Civil War.

903. Americans owe more than 785 million dollars in credit card debt.

904. After retiring from bank robbery, Frank James worked as a shoe salesman.

905. A person must average approximately 15 miles per hour to run a four minute mile.

906. Author Norman Mailer repeatedly stabbed and almost killed his second wife Adele, during an altercation in their apartment in 1960.

907. Gerald Ford, who lived to the age of 93 years and 165 days, is the longest-lived president in U.S. history.

908. 90% of the world's cinnamon is produced in Sri Lanka.

909. Lionnesses, female lions, do the majority of the hunting among lion prides.

910. Indonesia is the fourth most populous nation in the world.

911. Cow and pig skins are the primary ingredients in the manufacture of gelatin.

912. English Prime Minister Winston Churchill was nominated for both the Nobel Peace Prize and the Nobel Prize for Literature during his lifetime. He won the Prize for Literature in 1953.

913. Sap from the roots of the marshmallow plant has been used in sore throat-soothing candies since the time of the ancient Egyptians. Modern marshmallows contain absolutely no marshmallow plant ingredients.

914. Both U.S. President Benjamin Harrison and South Korean Prime Minister Chung Un-chan earned college degrees from Miami University of Ohio.

915. The largest of the giant redwood trees in California contain over 42,000 cubic feet of wood.

916. Nearly 30% of Kentuckians smoke cigarettes, the highest percentage of any state in the U.S.

917. Theodore Geisel, better known as Dr. Seuss, wrote an Academy Award winning documentary film about World War II, called *Design for Death*.

918. Sodium benzoate, a popular additive to soft drinks, fruit juices, salad dressing and other food products, is also used extensively as fuel for fireworks.

919. 80% of the nation of Greece is mountainous.

920. In 1922, the British Empire governed approximately 1/4 of the entire world's land surface.

921. Fish can yawn.

922. The Jacuzzi was invented in the U.S. by a family of Italian immigrants with the surname Jacuzzi.

923. Most of the animals killed by lions are strangled.

924. As a child, composer Johann Brahms earned money by playing piano in barrooms and brothels in

Germany.

925. A smash shot in table tennis can reach a speed of over 100 mph.

926. The temperature at Antarctica's Vostok Station reached -89.2 C/-128.6 F on July 21, 1983, the coldest temperature ever recorded on earth.

927. The first microwave oven stood almost six feet tall and weighed 750 pounds.

928. Campbell's Soup employee Donald Goerke helped develop over 100 products for the company, including SpaghettiOs and Chunky Soup.

929. U.S. park ranger Roy Sullivan was struck by lightning seven times during his lifetime.

930. Albert Einstein was a member of the NAACP.

931. The New York Stock Exchange began with an agreement among a small group of stock brokers meeting beneath a buttonwood tree in Manhattan in 1792.

932. The Hubble space telescope has been in almost continual use since its launch in April of 1990.

933. The originator of A1 Steak Sauce stole the original recipe from a chef.

934. A skunk can spray five or six times before reloading.

935. More than 160 million people use marijuana annually.

936. A scorpion will glow under black light.

937. Baltimore, Maryland, St. Louis, Missouri and Carson City, Nevada are all independent cities which do not belong to a county.

938. Western Union introduced the first credit card in 1921.

939. At more than 58,000 students, Arizona State University has the largest on-campus enrollment in the United States.

940. The first attempt on the life of a U.S. president occurred when a house painter named Richard Lawrence attempted, but failed, to shoot President Andrew Jackson in South Carolina in 1835.

941. Before King William I of England was known by the name William the Conqueror, he was known as William the Bastard.

942. A secret agreement was made between French and Canadian officials for the dismantlement and temporary relocation of the Eiffel Tower to Montreal for the World Expo in 1967. The agreement was never consummated.

943. John Paul Jones led an American attack on the English port of Whitehaven during the American Revolutionary War in 1778.

944. The 2009 salary of the Vice President of the United States, the Chief Justice of the Supreme Court and the Speaker of the House was $237,300 each.

945. Americans eat 70 million pounds of Tater Tots every year.

946. A cheetah can run up to 75 mph, and can go from 0 to 60 in less than three seconds.

947. Ballet originated as a dance interpretation of the sport of fencing.

948. Founded in 1744, Sotheby's auction house is the oldest company listed on the New York Stock Exchange.

949. Harry Truman was the last United States president to have never earned a college degree.

950. There are more than one million documented species of insects living on earth.

951. During Word War II, the Louisville Slugger company manufactured billy clubs for the U.S. Army.

952. Over 5,300 banks were robbed in the U.S. in 2009.

953. The writer O. Henry (William Sydney Porter) was the first to use the term "Banana Republic" in describing a Latin American nation with an unstable government. Porter coined the term while living in Honduras, after fleeing indictment for financial fraud by the U.S. government.

954. There are over two million tractor trailer units operating on U.S. highways.

955. Monarch butterflies have been known to complete transatlantic flights from North America to Europe.

956. It cost over two billion dollars to fund Project Manhattan, which produced the world's first atomic bomb in 1945.

957. The autograph of Button Gwinnett, who signed the Declaration of Independence on behalf of the Georgia delegation, is the most valuable autograph of

any American in history. His signature has brought as much as $150,000 at auction.

958. In 2010, there were officially 266 sovereign nations in the world.

959. In 2009, an estimated 84.24 million barrels of oil were produced every day. During the same year 83.62 million barrels of oil were consumed every day.

960. George Armstrong Custer's younger brother, Thomas, was awarded two Medals of Honor for his actions during the U.S. Civil War.

961. There are 35 bathrooms in the White House.

962. Mary Walker, a surgeon during the U.S. Civil War, is the nation's only female Medal of Honor winner.

963. U.S. military bases cover almost 30% of the total land area of the island of Guam.

964. Yellowjacket nests can have a population of up to 100,000 wasps.

965. Eight people were killed during the Green Corn Rebellion, a socialist uprising against the U.S. military draft in rural Oklahoma in 1917.

966. Lions typically rest for around 20 hours each day.

967. Franklin D. Roosevelt was named *Time* magazine's Person of the Year a record three times: in 1932, 1934 and 1941.

968. More than 7,200 people were killed in the three days of fighting that raged at the Battle of Gettysburg during the American Civil War.

969. More than 88 million passengers pass through Atlanta's Hartfield-Jackson Airport each year, more than any other airport in the world.

970. Soldier termites have such enlarged jaws that they cannot feed themselves. The soldiers are fed by the worker termites whom they defend from ant attacks.

971. King Philip II of Spain offered the modern equivalent of 6.5 million dollars in reward money for the life of English privateer Sir Francis Drake, in the 16th century.

972. The longest recorded flight time of a paper airplane is 27.6 seconds.

973. Cheyenne, Wyoming, is pelted with more hail storms per year than any other city in the United

States.

974. Michael Jackson's *Thriller* is the best-selling album of all time.

975. The Giant African Snail can grow to a weight of 2 pounds.

976. There are more than 2 million people in prison in the United States.

977. Upon the first successful test of the atomic bomb in 1945, scientist J. Robert Oppenheimer quoted the ancient Hindu text Bhagavad Gita: "...Now, I am become Death, the destroyer of worlds."

978. A volcano lies buried 2,900 feet below the city of Jackson, Mississippi.

979. An average rhinoceros lives to the age of 60 years.

980. Both Theodore Roosevelt and his son, Theodore Roosevelt Jr., were awarded the U.S. Medal of Honor.

981. An estimated 490,000 babies are born every day.

982. In 2009, highway drivers on the island of Samoa

switched from driving on the right side of the road to the left.

983. Over 40 million people visit Minnesota's Mall of America every year.

984. Betty Crocker is a fictional person.

985. A single female cricket can produce up to 2,000 baby crickets.

986. General George Patton competed, and placed fifth overall, in the modern pentathlon competition at the 1912 Summer Olympics in Stockholm.

987. The Apollo 10 command module reached a top speed of 24,790 miles per hour during its return from space in 1969.

988. There are more than 3,000 satellites in orbit above the earth.

989. In Medieval Europe, barbers not only cut hair but also performed surgeries and dental work.

990. A 650 pound catfish was caught in Thailand in 2005.

991. It took 21 years for workers to complete the

construction of the Taj Mahal.

992. Opossums are completely immune to rattlesnake venom.

993. Dolphins living in the hazardous Indus River sleep in intervals of between 4 and 60 seconds at a time.

994. Somewhere between 1.5 and 4 million people were killed, wounded or sickened because of the 872-day Siege of Leningrad by the Nazis during World War II.

995. The Apollo 11 astronauts were quarantined for 18 days following their return from the moon in 1969.

996. U.S. President Barack Obama owed $1,792,414 in federal income tax in 2009.

997. Baseball legend Ted Williams served as astronaut John Glenn's wing man in U.S. Air Force combat missions during the Korean War.

998. Three United States presidents graduated from Virginia's William and Mary College.

999. Charles Rolls, co-founder of luxury car maker Rolls-Royce, became Great Britain's first air fatality when he died flying a plane built by the Wright

brothers in 1910.

1000. It is estimated that every day for 20 years, 80 tons of stone were used to construct the Great Pyramid of Giza in Egypt.